Scope Note

Global Water Security

This is an IC-coordinated paper.

This report—requested by the Department of State—is designed to answer the question: How will water problems (shortages, poor water quality, or floods) impact US national security interests over the next 30 years? We selected 2040 as the endpoint of our research to consider longer-term impacts from growing populations, climate change, and continued economic development. However, we sometimes cite specific time frames (e.g., 2030, 2025) when reporting is based on these dates. For the Key Judgments, we emphasize impacts that will occur within the next 10 years.

We provide an introductory discussion of the global water picture, but we do not do a comprehensive analysis of the entire global water landscape. For the core classified analysis—a National Intelligence Estimate—we focused on a finite number of states that are strategically important to the United States and transboundary issues from a selected set of water basins **(Nile, Tigris-Euphrates, Mekong, Jordan, Indus, Brahmaputra,** and **Amu Darya)**. We judge that these examples are sufficient to illustrate the intersections between water challenges and US national security.

Assumptions: We assume that water management technologies will mature along present rates and that no far-reaching improvements will develop and be deployed over the next 30 years. In addition, for several states, we assume that present water policies—pricing and investments in infrastructure—are unlikely to change significantly. Cultural norms often drive water policies and will continue to do so despite recent political upheavals. Finally, we assume that states with a large and growing economic capacity continue to make infrastructure investments and apply technologies to address their water challenges.

This effort relied on previously published Intelligence Community (IC) products, peer-reviewed research, and consultations with outside experts. The Defense Intelligence Agency (DIA) was the principal drafter with contributions from NGA, CIA, State/INR, and DOE.

Selected Water Definitions

Aquifer: a geologic formation that will yield water to a well in sufficient quantities to make withdrawal of water feasible for beneficial use; permeable layers of underground rock or sand that hold or transmit groundwater below the water table.

Consumptive use: water not available for reuse, due to reasons such as evapotranspiration, evaporation, incorporation into plant tissue, and infiltration into groundwater.

Evapotranspiration: the sum of evaporation and plant transpiration (release of water vapor) from the Earth's land surface to the atmosphere.

Fresh water: as used in this report, fresh water may be considered as water of sufficient quality to support its intended purpose—agriculture, electrical power generation, industrial processes, or human consumption.

Groundwater: water within the earth that supplies wells and springs; water in the zone of saturation where all openings in rocks and soil are filled, the upper surface of which forms the water table.

Human security: as used in this report, sufficient access to commodities (food, water) and environments (shelter, health care) necessary to sustain human life.

Interbasin transfer: the physical transfer of water from one watershed to another.

Surface water: water that flows in streams, rivers, natural lakes, wetlands, and reservoirs.

Trickle irrigation: method in which water drips to the soil from perforated tubes or emitters.

Virtual water: the water used (or consumed) in the development or production of a good or commodity, typically agricultural products.[a]

Water scarcity: when a country or region's annual water supply is less than 1,000 cubic meters per person per year.

Water problems: as used in this report, a condition of water shortage (where water demand exceeds water supply), poor water quality (inadequate for its intended use), or excessive water (floods).

Water management: as used in this report, pricing decisions, allocations of water based upon hydrological modeling, development of water infrastructure (e.g., dams, levies, canals, water treatment facilities), the use of water infrastructure to control water flow, trade of products with high water content, and effective transboundary water agreements.

Water stress: when a country's or region's annual water supply is less than 1,700 cubic meters per person per year (for reference, US per capita total water used is 2,500 cubic meters per year) or a high water withdrawal ratio (WWR). See foldout chart.

Water withdrawal ratio (WWR): total freshwater withdrawals as a fraction of surface and groundwater availability.

---

[a] In general, livestock products have a higher virtual water content than crop products. For example, the global average virtual water content of maize, wheat, and rice (husked) is 900, 1,300 and 3,000 m³/ton respectively, whereas the virtual water contents of chicken meat, pork, and beef are 3,900, 4,900 and 15,500 m³/ton respectively.

Water Distribution

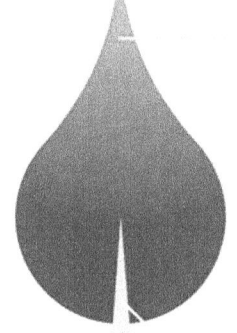

	percent
Oceans	**97.5**

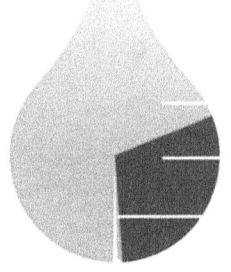

	percent
Fresh water	**2.5**

Glaciers	68.7
Groundwater	30.1
Permafrost	0.8

Surface and atmosphere	**0.4**

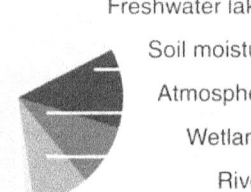

Freshwater lakes	67.5
Soil moisture	12.0
Atmosphere	9.5
Wetlands	8.5
Rivers	1.5
Vegetation	1.0

Freshwater Use

Sector usage of withdrawn water (consumptive and nonconsumptive)

Rivers, lakes, and groundwater

	percent
Agriculture	68
Domestic and other industrial	19
Power	10
Evaporation from reservoirs	3

Freshwater Use

Consumptive use of withdrawn water by sector

Rivers, lakes, and groundwater

	percent
Agriculture	93
Domestic and other industrial	7

Note: When humans use water, they affect the quantity, timing, or quality of water available to other users. Water for human use typically involves withdrawing water from lakes, rivers, or groundwater and either consuming it so that it reenters the atmospheric part of the hydrological cycle or returning it to the hydrological basin. When irrigated crops use water, it is consumptive use—it becomes unavailable for use elsewhere in the basin. In contrast, releasing water from a dam to drive hydroelectric turbines is generally a nonconsumptive use because the water is available for downstream users but not necessarily at the appropriate time. Withdrawals by a city for domestic and industrial use are mainly nonconsumptive, but if the returning water is inadequately treated, the quality of the water downstream is affected.

Source: Multiple, as quoted by World Bank, 2010.

Global Water Security

Key Judgments

Our Bottom Line: During the next 10 years, many countries important to the United States will experience water problems—shortages, poor water quality, or floods—that will risk instability and state failure, increase regional tensions, and distract them from working with the United States on important US policy objectives. Between now and 2040, fresh water availability will not keep up with demand absent more effective management of water resources. Water problems will hinder the ability of key countries to produce food and generate energy, posing a risk to global food markets and hobbling economic growth. As a result of demographic and economic development pressures, North Africa, the Middle East, and South Asia will face major challenges coping with water problems.

A. We assess that during the next 10 years, water problems will contribute to instability in states important to US national security interests. Water shortages, poor water quality, and floods by themselves are unlikely to result in state failure. However, water problems— when combined with poverty, social tensions, environmental degradation, ineffectual leadership, and weak political institutions— contribute to social disruptions that can result in state failure. We have moderate confidence in our judgment as we have reliable open source reporting on water pricing and infrastructure investments and reliable but incomplete all-source reporting on water quality.

The lack of adequate water will be a destabilizing factor in some countries because they do not have the financial resources or technical ability to solve their internal water problems. In addition, some states are further stressed by a heavy dependency on river water controlled by upstream nations with unresolved water-sharing issues. Wealthier developing countries probably will experience increasing water-related social disruptions but are capable of addressing water problems without risk of state failure.

B. We assess that a water-related state-on-state conflict is unlikely during the next 10 years. Historically, water tensions have led to more water-sharing agreements than violent conflicts. However, we judge that as water shortages become more acute beyond the next 10 years, water in shared basins will increasingly be used as leverage; the use of water as a weapon or to further terrorist objectives also will become more likely beyond 10 years. We have high confidence in our judgments because there are excellent all-source reports on future water shortages and a well-established pattern of water problems aggravating regional tensions.

We assess that during the next 10 years a number of states will exert leverage over their neighbors to preserve their water interests. This leverage will be applied in international forums and also include pressuring investors, nongovernmental organizations, and donor countries to support or halt water infrastructure projects.

- We assess that states will also use their inherent ability to construct and support major water projects to obtain regional influence or preserve their water interests. In addition, some nonstate actors (terrorists or extremists) almost certainly will target vulnerable water infrastructure to achieve their objectives.

C. We judge that during the next 10 years the depletion of groundwater supplies in some agricultural areas—owing to poor management—will pose a risk to both national and global food markets. We have high confidence in our judgment as we have numerous reliable open source projections on agricultural production and water depletion trends.

- Many countries have over-pumped their groundwater to satisfy growing food demand. Depleted and degraded groundwater can threaten food security and thereby risk social disruption. When water available for agriculture is insufficient, agricultural workers lose their jobs and fewer crops are grown. As a result, there is a strong correlation between water available for agriculture and national GDP.

- Over the long term, without mitigation actions (e.g., drip irrigation, reduction of distortive electricity-for-water pump subsidies, improved use of agricultural technology, and better food distribution networks), the exhaustion of groundwater sources will cause food production to decline and food demand will have to be satisfied through increasingly stressed global markets.

D. We assess that from now through 2040 water shortages and pollution probably will harm the economic performance of important trading partners. Economic output will suffer if countries do not have sufficient clean water supplies to generate electrical power or to maintain and expand manufacturing and resource extraction. Hydropower is an important source of electricity in developing countries—more than 15 developing countries generate 80 percent or more

of their electrical power from hydropower—and demand for water to support all forms of electricity production and industrial processes is increasing. We have moderate-to-high confidence in our judgment as we see no breakthrough technology that will reduce the industrial demand for water.

- In some countries, water shortages are already having an impact on power generation. Frequent droughts in other countries will undermine their long-term plans to increase current hydropower capacity.

E. We judge that, from now through 2040, improved water management (e.g., pricing, allocations, and "virtual water" trade) and investments in water-related sectors (e.g., agriculture, power, and water treatment) will afford the best solutions for water problems. Because agriculture uses approximately 70 percent of the global fresh water supply, the greatest potential for relief from water scarcity will be through technology that reduces the amount of water needed for agriculture. We have high confidence in this judgment because of the body of open source reporting indicating effective water management will be the most effective approach to mitigate water-related social tensions.

- Simple and inexpensive water management improvements in agriculture, including improved irrigation practices and land-leveling (to obtain an even distribution of water), are often the most straightforward way to compensate for increased demand and stretch existing water supplies.

Overview of Selected River Basins

River Basin	Type of Water Issue	Impact/Expected Time	River Basin Management Capacity[b]
Indus	• Poor water management • Inefficient agricultural practices • Soil salinization • Inadequate infrastructure • Greater variability in water availability • Water pollution	• Degraded regional food security—present to 2040 • Reduced resiliency to floods and droughts—present to 2040	Moderate
Jordan	• Depleted shared groundwater resources • Greater variability in water available • Water pollution • Poor coordination between countries	• Reduced resiliency to floods and drought—present to 2040 • Degraded regional food security—present to 2040 • Continuing regional tensions over water—present to 2040	Moderate
Mekong	• Increased development and demands • Greater variability in water available • Changes in sediment flows	• Reduced regional food security (to include fisheries) and negative impact on livelihoods—present to 2040 • Reduced resiliency to floods and droughts—present to 2040 • Increased regional tension over water development activity—present to 2040	Limited
Nile	• Decreasing per capita water available • Inadequate water agreements and management structure • Greater variability in water available • Water flow impeded as new dam reservoirs are filled • Delta erosion	• Degraded food security—present to 2040 • Reduced resiliency to floods and droughts—present to 2040 • Increased regional tensions over water and use of water as leverage—present to 2040	Limited
Tigris-Euphrates	• No multilateral water-sharing agreement. • Increased variability in water supply • Reduced water flow near-term • Altered sediment flows to downstream agricultural and marshlands	• Reduced resiliency to floods and droughts—present to 2040 • Reduced regional food security—present to 2040 • Continued regional tensions over unilateral water development projects and management—present to 2040	Limited
Amu Darya	• Inadequate water agreements • Degradation of water quality and disruption of flows some states • Poor water management	• Degraded regional food security—present to 2040 • Increased regional tensions over water—present to 2040 • Decreased health of populations around dried Aral Sea	Inadequate
Brahmaputra	• Uncoordinated land use and development plans • Insufficient water agreements • Reduced water flows • Saltwater intrusion into the delta	• Continuing regional tensions over unilateral water development projects—present to 2040 • Reduced potential for hydropower generation in some states—2020 to 2040 • Reduced regional food security, especially fisheries—present to 2040	Inadequate

---

[b] River basin management capacity is an assessment of the strength and resilience of institutional factors, such as treaties and river basin organizations that can provide stability, increase cooperation, and mitigate political grievances over water. However, even well-prepared river basins are likely to be challenged by increased water demand and impacts from climate change, which probably will lead to greater variability in extreme events.

Risks and Opportunities

Risks. Engineering solutions to water shortages—including the transfer of water between rivers—are becoming increasingly common, particularly as urban water demands grow. However, such measures threaten to raise tensions between organizations implementing these transfers and those harmed by them. In addition, in developing nations significant engineering efforts often harm the livelihoods of local populations, leading to increased poverty and food insecurity. They are expensive and degrade natural processes such as water cleaning and flood and drought mitigation. The lack of water data systems, especially in the developing world, leaves efforts to foster efficient water management open to the risk of creating unintended consequences through ignorance of the freshwater systems they are altering.

Opportunities. Because US expertise in water management is widely recognized, the developing world will look to the United States to lead the global community toward the development and implementation of sound policies for managing water resources at the local, national, and regional levels. Pressure will arise for a more engaged United States to make water a global priority and to support major development projects, including through financial assistance.

- US expertise on water resource management in both the public and private sectors is highly regarded and will be sought after worldwide. Improving water management, trade of products with high water content, and institutional capacities to treat water and encourage efficient water use will likely be the most effective approaches to mitigate water-related social tensions.

- States with water problems will require integrated water, land use, and economic data to achieve sound policymaking and management. The United States will be expected to develop and disseminate satellite and other remote sensing data and hydrological modeling tools that allow users to better understand and manage their resources.

- These states will look to the United States for support to develop legal and institutional arrangements that resolve water disputes or advance cooperative management of shared waters. Currently, water basin agreements often do not exist or are inadequate for many nations sharing watersheds. New or updated international agreements would lessen the risk of regional tensions over water.

- The United States can benefit from an increased demand for agricultural exports as water scarcity increases in various parts of the world. This would be especially true if states expecting increased water scarcity rely upon open markets instead of seeking bilateral land-lease arrangements in other countries to achieve their food security.

Contents

	Page
Scope Note	
Key Judgments	iii
Risks and Opportunities	vi
Discussion	1
Introduction—The Global Water Picture	1
Water Shortages	1
…and Poor Water Management	2
Other Water Problems	2
Impacts of Water Problems	3
Potential Water-Related Social Disruption and State Failures…	3
Potential Driver of Conflict or Political Tool	3
Water Pressures	4
Risks to Agriculture and Economic Growth	5
Water-Energy-Industry Nexus	6
Improving Water Management and Investments	6
Use of Technology and Infrastructure	7
Trade of Products with High Water Content ("Virtual Water")	8
Adoption of Pricing Mechanisms and Policies To Encourage Efficient Water Use	10
Hydrological Modeling for New and Revised Water-Sharing Agreements	10
Implications for the United States	11
Annex	
What We Mean When We Say: An Explanation of Estimative Language	13

This Assessment was prepared under the auspices of the Director of the Strategic Futures Group and drafted by the Defense Intelligence Agency. It was coordinated with the Intelligence Community.

This page has been intentionally left blank.

FRONT PAGE OF FOLDOUT

Global Water: Present to 2025

798325

BACK PAGE OF FOLDOUT

Discussion

Our Bottom Line: During the next 10 years, many countries important to the United States will experience water problems—shortages, poor water quality, or floods—that will risk instability and state failure, increase regional tensions, and distract them from working with the United States on important US policy objectives. Between now and 2040, fresh water availability will not keep up with demand absent more effective management of water resources. Water problems will hinder the ability of key countries to produce food and generate energy, posing a risk to global food markets and hobbling economic growth. As a result of demographic and economic development pressures, North Africa, the Middle East, and South Asia will face major challenges coping with water problems.

Introduction—The Global Water Picture

During the next 10 years, many countries important to the United States will almost certainly experience water problems—shortages, poor water quality, or floods—that will contribute to the risk of instability and state failure, and increase regional tensions. Additionally, states will focus on addressing internal water-related social disruptions which will distract them from working with the United States on important policy objectives.

Water Shortages

Between now and 2040, global demand for fresh water will increase, but the supply of fresh water will not keep pace with demand absent more effective management of water resources. A major international study finds that annual global water requirements will reach 6,900 billion cubic meters (bcm) in 2030, 40 percent above current sustainable water supplies. Climate change will cause water shortages in many areas of the world.

- The 2007 United Nations Intergovernmental Panel on Climate Change (IPCC) Assessment Report projects that by mid-century, annual river runoff and water availability will increase by 20-40 percent at high latitudes and in some wet tropical areas, and decrease by 10-30 percent over some dry regions at mid-latitudes and in the dry tropics, some of which are presently water-stressed areas. In the course of the century, water supplies stored in glaciers and snow cover are projected to decline, reducing water availability in regions supplied by meltwater from major mountain ranges. According to the IPCC, semi-arid and arid areas are particularly exposed to the impacts of climate change on water resources. Many of these areas (e.g., Mediterranean Basin, western United States, southern Africa, northeast Brazil, southern and eastern Australia) almost certainly will suffer a decrease in water resources due to climate change.

- We judge that mismanagement of water resources—especially groundwater overdrafts and wasteful agricultural irrigation practices—will exacerbate the supply problem in many regions.

Increasing Demand. Population increases, migration, and changing human consumption patterns resulting from economic growth will be key drivers of rising fresh water demand. World population is projected to grow by about 1.2 billion between 2009 and 2025—from 6.8 billion to near 8 billion people. The developing world, with its rapidly expanding urban centers, will see

1

the biggest increases in water demand, as its population grows larger and more affluent. Migrations to cities will drive major increases in water demand for personal consumption, sanitation, industry, and hydroelectric power. Urban and more affluent populations will demand greater quantities of water-intensive products with diets that contain more meats and fewer grains.

- Agriculture, which accounts for approximately 3,100 bcm, or just under 70 percent of global water withdrawals today, will, if current practices and efficiencies continue, require 4,500 bcm—65 percent of all water withdrawals—by 2030.

...but Declining Supply. According to the 2030 Water Resources Group (WRG), one-third of the world's population will live near water basins where the water deficit will be larger than 50 percent by 2030. A number of countries (or regions within countries) are already experiencing high "water stress"—when the annual renewable freshwater supplies are below 1,700 cubic meters per person per year.[c] Such areas include the western United States, northern Africa, southern Africa, the Middle East, Australia and parts of south Asia and China.

- By 2025, ISciences projects that water stress will increase significantly in many locations throughout the world, including north Africa, the Middle East, and Asia (see foldout).

With more than one-sixth of the Earth's population relying on meltwater from glaciers and seasonal snowpacks for their water supply, reductions in meltwater caused by climate change induced receding glaciers and reduced snow packs will have significant impacts.

- In the Andes, glacial meltwater supports river flows and water supplies for tens of millions of people during the long dry season. Many small glaciers will disappear within the next few decades, adversely affecting people and ecosystems. Hundreds of millions of people in Asia depend upon glacial meltwater from the Hindu Kush and Himalayas.

...and Poor Water Management

Inefficient water consumption as well as changing land-use patterns, such as deforestation and soil grading, will reduce the supply of water that would otherwise be available. Poor infrastructure in cities, with leakage rates between 30-50 percent[d], almost certainly will also diminish supplies, as will evaporation from manmade reservoirs. Other contributing factors include inadequate knowledge of ground and surface water budgets; unsatisfactory representations of water's value in economic models; and the lack of a generally agreed understanding of water rights. These factors increase the difficulty of managing water effectively within states and hinder the forging of effective water-sharing agreements between states.

Other Water Problems

In addition to water shortages, countries important to United States will have to cope with poor water quality and the impact of floods. The IPCC report states that the risk of drought and floods will increase markedly in many areas of the world by the end of the century owing to an increase in extreme weather events. During the next few decades rising sea levels and deteriorating coastal buffers will amplify the destructive power of coastal storms, including surges and heavy precipitation. At times water flows will be severe enough to overwhelm the water control infrastructures of even developed

---

[c] For reference, US per capita total water used is 2,500 cubic meters per person per year. Water stress is also often expressed as a high water withdrawal ration (WWR) (see foldout).

---

[d] For reference, 25-30 percent leakage is not uncommon for older US cities (i.e., Detroit, Philadelphia); hydrologists consider leakage of 15 percent as normal or good.

countries, including the United States. The challenge will be greater in urban areas of the developing world where flood-control infrastructures are often poorly maintained.

Drinking water from both aquifers and surface water resources almost certainly will further decline in many areas of the developing world, as water quality decreases from salt-water intrusion and industrial, biofuel, agricultural, and sanitation processes.

Impacts of Water Problems

KJ A. We assess that during the next 10 years, water problems will contribute to instability in states important to US national security interests. Water shortages, poor water quality, and floods by themselves are unlikely to result in state failure. However, water problems—when combined with poverty, social tensions, environmental degradation, ineffectual leadership, and weak political institutions—contribute to social disruptions that can result in state failure. We have moderate confidence in our judgment as we have reliable open source reporting on water pricing and infrastructure investments and reliable but incomplete all-source reporting on water quality.

- The lack of adequate water will be a destabilizing factor in some countries because they do not have the financial resources or technical ability to solve their internal water problems. In addition, some states are further stressed by a heavy dependency on river water controlled by upstream nations with unresolved water-sharing issues. Wealthier developing countries probably will experience increasing water-related social disruptions but are capable of addressing water problems without risk of state failure.

Potential Water-Related Social Disruptions and State Failures...

States at Risk. We judge that over the next 10 years, water shortages, and government failures to manage them, are likely to lead to social disruptions, pressure on national and local leaders, and potentially political instability. Social disruptions eventually leading to state failure are plausible when the population believes water shortages are the result of poor governance, hoarding, or control of water by elites and other destabilizing factors are present.

Some States Better Able To Cope. Large developing countries will face water problems that will vary significantly across their territory. However, given their geographic position, economic strength, and capacity to engineer solutions, we assess the risk is low that social disruptions will lead to state failure in these countries. Nevertheless, central and regional governments will be preoccupied with managing water problems.

Potential Driver of Conflict or Political Tool

KJ B. We assess that a water-related state-on-state conflict is unlikely during the next 10 years. Historically, water tensions have led to more water-sharing agreements than violent conflicts. However, we judge that as water shortages become more acute beyond the next 10 years, water in shared basins will increasingly be used as leverage; the use of water as a weapon or to further terrorist objectives also will become more likely beyond 10 years. We have high confidence in our judgments because there are excellent all-source reports on future water shortages and a well-established pattern of water problems aggravating regional tensions. Fluctuating water availability and relative scarcity of natural resources have been cited by scholars as a factor in political conflict and even war.

Water as a Driver for Peace

Water challenges have often brought divergent actors together to resolve a common problem. Once cooperative water agreements are established through treaties, they are often resilient over time and produce peaceful cooperation, even among other existing hostilities and contentious issues.

- The Mekong Committee, established by Cambodia, Laos, Thailand, and Vietnam in 1957 exchanged data and information on the river basin throughout the Vietnam War.

- Israel and Jordan held secret "picnic table" talks to manage the Jordan River starting in 1953, even though they were officially at war from 1948 until 1994.

- The Indus River Commission survived two major wars between India and Pakistan.

In some cases, joint water governance has created cooperation on broader issues. Water can serve as a potential entry point for peace and support sustainable cooperation among nations.

Water as Leverage. We assess that during the next 10 years a number of states will exert leverage over their neighbors to preserve their water interests. This leverage will be applied in international forums and also include pressuring investors, nongovernmental organizations, and donor countries to support or halt water infrastructure projects. Additionally, we assess that states will also use their inherent ability to construct and support major water projects to obtain regional influence or preserve their water interests.

Water as a Weapon. We judge that the use of water as a weapon will become more common during the next 10 years with more powerful upstream nations impeding or cutting off downstream flow. Water will also be used within states to pressure populations and suppress separatist elements.

Water Terrorism. Physical infrastructure, including dams, has been used as convenient and high-publicity targets by extremists, terrorists, and rogue states threatening substantial harm and will become more likely beyond the next 10 years. Even if an attack is less than fully successful, the fear of massive floods or loss of water resources would alarm the public and cause governments to take costly measures to protect the water infrastructure.

Desalinization facilities or critical single point failure water canals or pipelines would likewise be targets for terrorists.

Water Pressures

If water problems are not managed successfully, food supplies will decline, energy available for economic growth will be reduced, and the risk of certain diseases will increase (see textbox on page 5). We assess that water stresses contribute to or aggravate existing problems such as poverty, social tensions, environmental degradation, ineffectual leadership, and weak political institutions.

- Universal access to water and sanitation are included in the UN Millennium Development Goals (MDGs)—a global activity plan to achieve anti-poverty goals by 2015. The World Bank estimates that even if countries develop policies and improve water institutions, the additional external foreign aid required to reach the Water and Sanitation MDGs by 2015 is between USD $5-21 billion.

Increased Risk of Disease

Water scarcity—driven in part by poor or inadequate water infrastructure—forces populations to rely on unsafe sources of drinking water, increasing the risk of waterborne diseases such as cholera, dysentery, and typhoid fever. During the dry season, as water supplies (including ground- and surface water) become more limited, concentrated pathogenic organisms increase the chance for outbreaks of waterborne diseases. These dry season outbreaks typically portend explosive transmission of waterborne diseases—particularly cholera—in the rainy season when the total quantity of pathogen in the environment dramatically increases. Furthermore, water diversion projects (e.g., dams, reservoirs, and irrigation systems) cause waters to be stagnant or slow-moving, which creates favorable conditions for increased populations of disease-transmitting vectors such as mosquitoes (e.g., dengue, malaria), flies (e.g., onchocerciasis), snails (e.g., schistosomiasis), or copepods (e.g., Guinea worm). Water scarcity, and the inability to wash, directly results in skin infections and trachoma, the leading cause of preventable blindness. In general, water scarcity-related diseases will disproportionately sicken poorer populations in developing countries, leading to decreased economic productivity, missed educational opportunities, and high health care costs.

- On average, a child dies from a water-related disease every 15 seconds, according to a 2006 United Nations Human Development Report. Unsafe drinking water and poor sanitation are leading causes of death in the developing world for children under age 5. Close to half of all people living in developing nations are suffering from a health problem related to water and sanitation deficits.

- The cholera outbreak in Haiti was initially propagated by a concentrated contamination of the Artibonite River during low flow levels. During the rainy and hurricane season of 2010, cholera spread nationwide, further contaminating drinking water supplies. As of 30 September 2011, more than 455,000 Haitians had been treated for cholera, 242,000 were hospitalized, and 6,400 died.

- Trachoma—which threatens 400 million individuals with blindness and is prevalent in children—is a direct result of dry, dusty water-scarce environments where sanitation is lacking, according to the World Health Organization.

Risks to Agriculture and Economic Growth

KJ C. We judge that during the next 10 years the depletion of groundwater supplies in some agricultural areas—owing to poor management—will pose a risk to both national and global food markets. We have high confidence in our judgment as we have numerous reliable open source projections on agricultural production and water depletion trends. Numerous countries have over-pumped their groundwater to satisfy growing food demand. Depleted and degraded groundwater can threaten food security and thereby risk social disruption. When water available for agriculture is insufficient, agricultural workers lose their jobs and fewer crops are grown. As a result, there is a strong correlation between water available for agriculture and national GDP. Over the long term, without mitigation actions (e.g., drip irrigation, reduction of distortive electricity-for-water pump subsidies, improved use of agricultural technology, and better food distribution networks), the exhaustion of groundwater sources will cause food production to decline and food demand will have to be satisfied through increasingly stressed global markets.

- In developing countries, annual precipitation fluctuations shape water available for agriculture and can determine crop production.

- Currently, 35 percent of the global labor force is employed in agriculture, with a higher percentage in many developing countries, where agriculture accounts for as much as 95 percent of total water use, according to the UN Food and Agriculture Organization (FAO).

Many advances in agricultural production have been due to the unprecedented use of finite groundwater reserves. An estimated 99 percent of the Earth's accessible fresh water is found in aquifers, and about 2 billion people rely on groundwater as their sole source of water. Some groundwater is located in aquifers that are not renewable (fossil aquifers); in other cases, water extraction from aquifers exceeds the replenishment rate. Certain groundwater systems need multiple centuries to replenish. Total annual overdrafts from aquifers around the world are probably double the annual flow of the Nile River.

- Based upon NASA satellite data, water is being depleted faster in northern India than in any other comparable region in the world. The World Bank assesses that groundwater irrigation directly or indirectly supports 60 percent of irrigated agriculture, and 15 percent of India's food production depends on unsustainable groundwater use, according to a 2005 World Bank study citing a 1999 Indian report.

Water-Energy-Industry Nexus

KJ D. We assess that from now through 2040 water shortages and pollution probably will harm the economic performance of important trading partners. Economic output will suffer if countries do not have sufficient clean water supplies to generate electrical power or to maintain and expand manufacturing and resource extraction. Hydropower is an important source of electricity in developing countries—more than 15 developing countries generate 80 percent or more of their electrical power from hydropower—and demand for water

to support all forms of electricity production and industrial processes is increasing. We have moderate-to-high confidence in our judgment as we see no breakthrough technology that will reduce the industrial demand for water.

- In some countries, water shortages are already having an impact on power generation. Frequent droughts in other countries will undermine their long-term plans to increase current hydropower capacity.

Improving Water Management and Investments

KJ E. We judge that, from now through 2040, improved water management[e] (e.g., pricing, allocations, and "virtual water" trade) and investments in water-related sectors (e.g., agriculture, power, and water treatment) will afford the best solutions for water problems. Because agriculture uses approximately 70 percent of the global fresh water supply, the greatest potential for relief from water the greatest potential for relief from water scarcity will be through technology that reduces the amount of water needed for agriculture. We have high confidence in this judgment because of the body of open source reporting indicating effective water management will be the most effective approach to mitigate water-related social tensions. Effective water management has several components:

- Use of an integrated water resource management framework that assesses the whole ecosystem and then uses technology and infrastructure for efficient water use, flood control, redistribution of water, and preservation of water quality.

---

[e] Water management includes pricing decision, allocations of water based upon hydrological modeling, development of water infrastructure (dams, levies, canals, water treatment facilities, etc.), the use of water infrastructure to control water flow, trade of products with high water content, and effective transboundary water agreements.

Biofuels

Biofuels are often seen as a renewable carbon-neutral alternative to fossil fuels. Current biofuel development requires water and aggravates water scarcity. Access to water will become a primary factor in the development of biofuel feedstock production. At present, biofuel production uses a small fraction of both agricultural land and transportation fuel supply. The biomass needed to produce one liter of biofuel (under currently available conversion techniques) consumes between 1,000 and 3,500 liters of water, on a global average, according to the "Comprehensive Assessment of Water Management in Agriculture" published by Earthscan and the Colombo International Water Institute. The World Bank reports land allocated to biofuels is projected to increase fourfold by 2030, with most of the growth in North America (accounting for 10 percent of arable land) and Europe (15 percent of arable land). In the developing world, research projections indicate that a small amount of arable land will be dedicated to biofuel production by 2030: 0.4 percent in Africa; 3 percent in Asia; and 3 percent Latin America.

- Trade of products with high water content to overcome inherent local water deficiencies.

- Adoption of pricing mechanisms and policies to encourage efficient water use and support infrastructure investments.

- More robust remote- sensing/river-gauging networks and hydrological modeling to support new and revised water-sharing agreements.

Use of Technology and Infrastructure

Although no breakthrough technology advances to address water problems are expected to emerge and be deployed in the next 10 years, technology will make important contributions in niche areas over the next 30 years. (See textbox on page 9.) Proper use of existing technology can increase the efficiency of water used in agriculture, electrical power generation, and industrial processes; and improve water quality, distribution, and flood control.

- The use of existing technology for conservation and efficiency—particularly in agriculture—offers the best hope to increase human security and facilitate economic growth. Enhancing irrigation performance promises better yields, but it will still be necessary to increase global water withdrawals by nearly a third.

- Simple and inexpensive water management improvements in agriculture, including improved irrigation practices and land-leveling (to obtain an even distribution of water), are often the most straight forward way to compensate for increased demand and stretch existing water supplies. In the Amu Darya Basin for example, improved water management practices, such as land leveling, could annually save 2,000 cubic meters of water for each of the 4 million hectares of irrigated area, totaling about 8 billion cubic meters throughout the basin.

- In the case of China, according to the Water Resources Group, even though 50 percent of water is used in agriculture, the largest growth rate in water use is seen in the industrial and domestic sectors. Therefore, investments in water efficiency and water treatment primarily for industrial water use would fill China's water gap through 2030 and reduce operating costs more than enough to offset these investments.

Infrastructure/Environmental Tradeoffs

We judge that over time, water infrastructure planning led by nongovernmental organizations has shifted from an emphasis on water management efficiency to an emphasis on environmental preservation of ecosystem services. The message to the developing world is that environmental protection takes priority over development because there is a lack of understanding and education related to the functionality and services provided by river systems. This approach often leads to missed opportunities for engagement and less sustainable development, as developing countries work bilaterally with countries willing to provide development assistance.

Neglecting infrastructure investments (e.g., dams, canals, and water management sensors) can also increase vulnerability to extreme weather events. Studies have shown that water investments reduce damages from extreme weather events from 25-30 percent of GDP to around 5 percent, making these investments a crucial element in achieving social stability.

In the interest of near-term development, states have often sacrificed the preservation of water quality and initiated major water infrastructure or industrial projects. This change in the allocation of funding for local water resources has often resulted in social disruptions.

Hydropower dams can boost development, but also block most of the sediment and nutrient flows downstream needed to maintain and nourish the rivers and deltas, a crucial source for agriculture production and fish.

- Engineering solutions to water shortages—including the transfer of water between rivers—are becoming increasingly common, particularly as urban water demands grow. However, such measures also threaten to raise tensions between entities implementing these transfers and those hurt by them. More effective data systems are required, especially in the developing world, to foster efficient water management and build trust between parties.

Trade of Products with High Water Content ("Virtual Water")

The World Economic Forum forecasts that future water demand for many rapidly industrializing economies across South Asia, the Middle East, and North Africa—supporting approximately 2.5 billion people—can be met only through increased trade. Although water is not a commodity that is directly traded on the open market, it is vital in the production of food and other commodities that are traded globally. Global commodity prices incorporate the value of water ("virtual water") and other resource inputs used in production.

- The Middle East and North Africa have partially addressed their water shortages by purchasing high-water-content food commodities whose virtual water content is equivalent to having another Nile River flowing into the region. Increasing water shortages and rising food prices will present growing challenges for all but the wealthiest countries in these regions who can afford—typically with fossil fuel revenues—to subsidize food.

- The United States, Russia, and Canada, as major agriculture exporters, can benefit from an increased demand for their products, as water shortages increase in various parts of the world. This would be especially true if states, expecting increased water problems, rely upon open markets instead of seeking bilateral land-lease arrangements to achieve their food security.

Technology will have an important impact on fresh water supply and demand in the next 30 years, but changes will be evolutionary, according to a NIC-sponsored contractor study. Changes are expected in salt-tolerant crops and point-of-use applications for the safe human consumption of untreated water. Membrane and other nanotechnology applications that dominate the current desalination and water-purification industries are likely to account for the biggest advances and effects on fresh water availability. Although desalination may be economically feasible for household and industrial water, it is not currently feasible for agriculture. In providing new sources of water, any technology faces three hurdles: reducing energy consumption, lowering production costs, and eliminating the fouling of membranes and filters.

- Because all desalination processes produce a saline concentrate, the environmental impact of using or disposing of this concentrate also poses a hurdle.

- Given the low price of water charged in most regions of the world, users are less motivated to adopt technologies such as desalination and drip-irrigation systems. For industry and households, water prices in developed countries range from $0.60/cubic meter to more than $3/cubic meter. Water for agriculture in most countries is priced at approximately $0.10/cubic meter. Recent data indicate that desalination processes produce water at much higher costs: $0.61/cubic meter for reverse osmosis, and $0.72/cubic meter to $0.89/cubic meter for thermal processes.

Technology that reduces the amount of water needed for agriculture offers the greatest potential for relief from water shortages. Local point-of-use technologies can also provide safe drinking water in the developing world.

- Advances in large-scale drip-irrigation systems are the most likely approach to address water shortages for agriculture.

- Research to develop drought resistance in crops has been conducted for several decades, but no commercialization exists to date. During the next three decades, selected crops could be developed that require half the water used by current crops, but widespread cultivation of such crops is problematic.

- Limited experiments are being conducted to develop food plants that can tolerate salt or waste water. The advances in biotechnology may result in new plants or genetically altered strains that can grow in salt water from the ocean or large saltwater aquifers.

Point-of-use water-purification technology relies upon portable systems that tend to be self-contained. These systems are used by recreational enthusiasts and military personnel, and will be used by habitants in the developing world who must obtain drinking water from untreated sources (e.g., rivers, lakes). New technology is currently emerging in the commercial market, and evolutionary advances in lowering costs and fail-safe designs are likely. Point-of-use technology is not capable of supporting larger agricultural or industrial needs.

Adoption of Pricing Mechanisms and Policies To Encourage Efficient Water Use

Many economists advocate the privatization of water services to generate funds for water infrastructure and better manage water demands. However, properly run government water utilities can also provide excellent services and generate sufficient revenue to sustain their water infrastructure. Although water privatization has been successful in many countries, it can threaten established use patterns by increasing the costs of water or transferring ownership of water sources to private companies without proper local governance structures. Privatization also makes water supply vulnerable to market forces which can conflict with societal expectations. In many developing agricultural areas around the world, farmers pay nothing directly for water use and often view water charges as expropriation of water rights acquired with the land. Privatization can lead to instability, as people become unable to afford water and/or become restive as they perceive their right to water being threatened.

- With the help of aid agencies and development banks to improve the infrastructure and local decisions to install water meters and charge reasonable rates, the government-owned water utility in Phnom Penh, Cambodia, now makes a profit and pays taxes. The replacement of corrupt management with honest, competent management also contributed to the turnaround.

- In some portions of the Middle East, generation of financial revenue to make investments for basic water needs is limited by moral beliefs that water cannot be sold and only treatment and distribution costs may be recouped. Hence, the true cost for energy-intensive desalination efforts are not passed on to water customers. This causes extraordinary financial losses and reduces any desire for free market infrastructure reinvestment. Often a state's ability to provide water to its populace depends on heavy subsidies. Any reduction of those subsidies would risk social disruption, water production, or both.

Hydrological Modeling for New and Revised Water-Sharing Agreements

We judge that as global water demands increase, many nations included within the 263 shared international water basins worldwide would benefit from new or updated international agreements. Effective water agreements encourage greater cooperation and lessen the risk of regional conflicts. Today, water basin agreements often do not exist or are inadequate. Additionally, the absence of good hydrological modeling and water flow/level measurements (from on the ground or via remote sensors) creates distrust among nations sharing a common basin. Shortcomings in water basin agreements often further enable stronger states to preserve their influence over weaker states.

- Water-sharing agreements are often complicated by changes to the larger political structure. After the collapse of the Soviet Union, management and sharing of the Amu Darya and Syr Darya Rivers became contentious. Barter arrangements, which involved trading cheap fuel and electricity provided by downstream countries for water released by upstream countries, were interrupted.

- In South Asia, three distinct treaties, adopting different approaches, cover the Indus, Ganges, and Mahakali Rivers. The Indus Waters Treaty divides the basin, giving the three western branches of the river to Pakistan and the three eastern branches to India. The Ganges Treaty governs the sharing of the river water between India and Bangladesh, stipulating how much water each party should receive every 10 days during the yearly wet season between 1 January and 31 May. The Mahakali Treaty was intended for India and

Nepal to share the development of the river. Of the three agreements, only the Ganges River accord makes explicit provisions for substantial shortfalls in river flow of the kind that may occur from climate change-induced impacts on glacier melt or precipitation patterns.

The UN Convention on the Law of the Non-Navigational Uses of International Watercourses, adopted in 1997 by the UN General Assembly, is the foundation for most nations regarding the governance of international transboundary water resources. Although the UN Convention and international law offer general guidance to co-riparian states (states that share a river basin), largely ineffective practical enforcement mechanisms and a lack of international ratification limit its effectiveness. To date, 14 years after its adoption by the UN General Assembly, the UN Watercourses Convention has only 24 contracting states, 11 short of that required for the convention to be entered into force.

Implications for the United States

Many states turn to the developed world to find alternative ways to meet their infrastructure needs. Water planners in developing countries regularly lack adequate data (hydrological models and actual water levels) for effective policymaking. For example, knowledge of water balances in specific tributaries, replenishment rates for shared aquifers, or water demands in particular communities may be either unavailable or inaccessible. The developing world will probably expect the United States, as a leader in technology, to continue development of hydrological models and remote environmental monitoring, as well as to disseminate this data and facilitate the integration of other terrestrial resource management data on a global scale. US technological capability in water treatment and purification and the efficient use of water in agriculture will also be sought after.

- Although the United States is recognized as a leader in water technology, other countries have identified research in water technology as a national priority and will challenge US leadership over time.

- The United States probably will be expected to continue the development and promotion of water management and agricultural technology and expertise, fostering management capacity and appropriately sharing technology.

Irrespective of other policies toward the United States, both developed and developing states will look for US support of international agreements, and institutions and national and subnational partners, seeking to improve water management. Active engagement by the United States to resolve water challenges will improve US influence and may forestall other actors achieving the same influence at US expense.

11

The US Water Experience

The development of water resources played a pivotal role in the development of the United States. Investments in water infrastructure helped build a regionally divided nation into one and transformed major regions from poverty to prosperity. The Pacific Northwest alone evolved from a poverty-stricken region in the 1930s to become one of the most economically successful regions in the world. The change was even more dramatic in the south with oversight from the Tennessee Valley Authority (TVA). By making water flow data freely available to all users, the United States sets an example noticed throughout the world. Domestic water disputes still arise, but they are addressed fairly and transparently. The United States is also one of the highest exporters of "virtual water" (water consumed in the manufacturing or growing of an export product), providing numerous opportunities for engagement with the rest of the world.

The unique 1964 agreement between Canada and the United States has guided the cooperative management of the Columbia River and provided benefits such as power generation, flood control, irrigation, and navigation that would not be available if each country acted independently. The treaty, which divides hydropower benefits and costs, led to the construction of three large storage dams in British Columbia. The dams are used for downstream flood control and power generation at the lower dams in the United States. The treaty will be reviewed in 2014 as part of a normal process that allows for the treaty to expire.

Although most of the Colorado River originates in the basin's upper states (i.e., Colorado, Utah, Wyoming), a 1922 Colorado River Compact allocates most of the water to the lower states (i.e., California, Arizona, Nevada, and New Mexico). Unfortunately, the agreement was based on data from the unseasonably wet five years prior to 1922, estimating the average flow to be 17.5 million acre-feet (maf). The actual average flow over the last 100 years has been nowhere near this number, averaging about 13 maf, with high variability ranging from 4.4 maf to over 22 maf. A 2009 study by the University of Colorado projects that all reservoirs along the Colorado River—which provide water for 27 million people—could dry up by 2057 because of climate change and overuse. More recently, drought and low Lake Mead water levels have resulted in a multi-billion dollar plan to build a 285-mile pipeline to pump groundwater to the Las Vegas area from as far away as Snake Valley, which straddles the Nevada-Utah state line.

A 1944 agreement between the United States and Mexico stipulates the terms of water-sharing between the two countries, with water delivery obligations on each side. The Colorado and Rio Grande Rivers, as well as their major tributaries, are covered in the agreement. The agreement allows the United States access to tributary contributions from Mexican rivers, and no Mexican access to contributions from US tributary rivers, and therefore many view the agreement as unfair. Delayed water deliveries, and even efforts to reduce canal water leakage, have occasionally complicated broader relations but have not been a major source of stress.

Annex

What We Mean When We Say: An Explanation of Estimative Language

We use phrases such as *we judge, we assess,* and *we estimate*—and probabilistic terms such as *probably* and *likely*—to convey analytical assessments and judgments. Such statements are not facts, proof, or knowledge. These assessments and judgments generally are based on collected information, which often is incomplete or fragmentary. Some assessments are built on previous judgments. In all cases, assessments and judgments are not intended to imply that we have "proof" that shows something to be a fact or that definitively links two items or issues.

In addition to conveying judgments rather than certainty, our estimative language also often conveys 1) our assessed likelihood or probability of an event; and 2) the level of confidence we ascribe to the judgment.

Estimates of Likelihood. Because analytical judgments are not certain, we use probabilistic language to reflect the Community's estimates of the likelihood of developments or events. Terms such as *probably, likely, very likely,* or *almost certainly* indicate a greater than even chance. The terms *unlikely* and *remote* indicate a less than even chance that an event will occur; they do not imply that an event will not occur. Terms such as *might* or *may* reflect situations in which we are unable to assess the likelihood, generally because relevant information is unavailable, sketchy, or fragmented. Terms such as *we cannot dismiss, we cannot rule out,* or *we cannot discount* reflect an unlikely, improbable, or remote event whose consequences are such that it warrants mentioning. The chart provides a rough idea of the relationship of some of these terms to each other.

Remote	Very Unlikely	Unlikely	Even chance	Probably Likely	Very Likely	Almost certainly

Confidence in Assessments. Our assessments and estimates are supported by information that varies in scope, quality and sourcing. Consequently, we ascribe *high, moderate,* or *low* levels of confidence to our assessments, as follows:

- *High confidence* generally indicates that our judgments are based on high-quality information, and/or that the nature of the issue makes it possible to render a solid judgment. A "high confidence" judgment is not a fact or a certainty, however, and such judgments still carry a risk of being wrong.

- *Moderate confidence* generally means that the information is credibly sourced and plausible but not of sufficient quality or corroborated sufficiently to warrant a higher level of confidence.

- *Low confidence* generally means that the information's credibility and/or plausibility is questionable, or that the information is too fragmented or poorly corroborated to make solid analytic inferences, or that we have significant concerns or problems with the sources.

This page has been intentionally left blank.

The National Intelligence Council manages the Intelligence Community's estimative process, incorporating the best available expertise inside and outside the government. It reports to the Director of National Intelligence in his capacity as head of the US Intelligence Community and speaks authoritatively on substantive issues for the Community as a whole.

Chairman	Christopher Kojm
Vice Chairman	Joseph Gartin
Counselor; Director, Analysis and Production Staff	Mathew J. Burrows
Chief of Staff	Mark Roth
Director, Strategic Futures Group	Casimir Yost
Senior Advisor, Global Health Security	Clyde Manning

National Intelligence Officers

Africa	Theresa Whelan
Cyber Issues	Sean Kanuck
East Asia	Paul Heer
Economic Issues	Roger Kubarych
Europe	Karen Donfried
Iran	Jillian Burns
Military Issues	John Landry
The Near East	Alan Pino
North Korea	Andrew Claster
Russia and Eurasia	Eugene Rumer
Science & Technology	Lawrence Gershwin
South Asia	Robert S. Williams
Transnational Threats	Julie Cohen
Weapons of Mass Destruction and Proliferation	Brian Lessenberry
The Western Hemisphere	Arthur Tuten, Acting

National Security Information

Information available as of October 2011 was used in the preparation of this product.

**The following intelligence organizations participated
in the preparation of this product:**

The Central Intelligence Agency

The Defense Intelligence Agency

The National Security Agency

The National Geospatial-Intelligence Agency

The Bureau of Intelligence and Research, Department of State

The Federal Bureau of Investigation

Office of Intelligence and Analysis, Department of Homeland Security

Office of the Director of National Intelligence, National Counterterrorism Center

Also participating:

The Office of the Director of National Intelligence, National Counterintelligence Executive

.

This page has been intentionally left blank.

ISBN 9781542975902